Wild About Wildlife

Have You Got What It Takes to Be a Zookeeper?

by Lisa Thompson

Compass Point Books ✦ Minneapolis, Minnesota

First American edition published in 2008 by
Compass Point Books
3109 West 50th Street, #115
Minneapolis, MN 55410

Editor: Mari Bolte
Designers: Lori Bye and Jaime Martens
Creative Director: Keith Griffin
Editorial Director: Nick Healy
Managing Editor: Catherine Neitge
Content Adviser: Jacque Blessington, Board Member,
              American Association of Zoo Keepers, Inc.
              Kansas City, Mo.

Editor's note: To best explain careers to readers, the author has
created composite characters based on extensive interviews and research.

 This book was manufactured with paper containing
at least 10 percent post-consumer waste.
Printed in the United States of America

Library of Congress Cataloging-in-Publication Data
Thompson, Lisa, 1969–
  Wild about wildlife : have you got what it takes to be a zookeeper? / by Lisa Thompson.
    p. cm. — (On the job)
  Includes index.
  ISBN 978-0-7565-3616-9 (library binding)
  1. Zoo keepers—Vocational guidance—Juvenile literature. I. Title. II. Series.
  QL50.5.T46 2008
  636.088'9023—dc22   2007032704

Visit Compass Point Books on the Internet at *www.compasspointbooks.com*
or e-mail your request to *custserv@compasspointbooks.com*

Table of Contents

Feeding Time at the Zoo

Everyone's waking up.

The zoo is alive this morning with the yawns of lions, gorillas, and hippos as I begin my shift as a zookeeper. It's 7 A.M., and my first job is to check on the animals in my area. I work in the Australian Outback exhibit at our zoo, where visitors can get an up-close look at wallabies, kangaroos, Tasmanian devils, and other Australian animals.

I make sure I look in on a little koala called Kaya. She has been losing weight and eating poorly for the past few weeks and we're not sure why.

We have been keeping a special eye on her, recording her weight, movement, feeding, and sleeping patterns. We usually don't give the animals this much hands-on treatment, but koalas, especially sick ones, require special care. Today the vet plans on examining Kaya to try to find out what's wrong and how we can help her.

The other animals seem fine, so I grab my cleaning gear—wheelbarrow, shovel, rake, broom, mop, hose, and disinfectant sprays—and get busy cleaning out the holding areas, where the animals are kept overnight. These areas all need to be sprayed, scrubbed, squeegeed, and dry-mopped before the zoo opens. I change the water in each animal's enclosure as well.

The animals know that after cleaning, it's breakfast time—so they're very excited to see me.

As usual, I am pleased to see them, but this morning I am a little distracted. My mind is on the zoo tour I am leading this afternoon, and I can't help thinking about Kaya and her mysterious lack of appetite. I will feel better when the vet has checked her over.

Suddenly I hear people shouting and pointing skyward. I look up to see that Ralph, our wedge-tailed eagle, has escaped and is circling above.

As I watch the eagle, keepers race to our rescue vehicle. Ralph was raised here in the zoo, so I don't like his chances of surviving outside. I wonder how he got out.

A Zookeeper's Job is Never Done

Although all zookeepers look after the animals in a zoo, they can also have other responsibilities. They may care for one kind of animal or a number of different animals, depending on their experience and the kind of exhibit they work in. They maintain the exhibits, including checking fencing and landscaping, keep the grounds looking tidy, and are in charge of other general upkeep. Making sure that the animals are happy and healthy is also important.

Other places to work

Caring for animals in captivity is not limited to zoos. Animal caretakers also work at wildlife parks, aquariums, theme parks, mobile animal displays, and rehabilitation centers.

Zookeepers have many tasks to do every day, such as:

- Prepare food for the animals
- Order and collect special foods for the animals that require it
- Check animals' weight and record their overall health

- Feed the animals—some young animals have to be fed as often as every two hours if their mothers can't feed them
- Watch animals closely and call the vet if they look ill
- Maintain exhibits
- Check animals' teeth
- Give talks to the public

- Treat scratches and cuts if animals have had a fight or an accident
- Check animals' feet; clip long nails or trim hooves if needed
- Participate in animal training and enrichment exercises
- Move animals to new enclosures or into night yards

Timetable of my typical day

7:30 A.M. Animal check—look for any abnormal behavior, illness, or injury. It is important to do a thorough check in the morning, since it has been several hours since they were last observed.
-Prepare and serve morning feed
-Clean outdoor exhibits

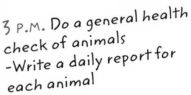

9 A.M. Move animals to their outdoor exhibit areas for zoo opening time
-Clean indoor holding areas

12:30–1:30 P.M. Lunchtime

1:30 P.M. Prepare afternoon meals and order feed for the following morning from the zoo's commissary area, where food is stored and prepared.

3 P.M. Do a general health check of animals
-Write a daily report for each animal

5 P.M. Move animals back to indoor/sleeping areas
-Serve afternoon feed
-Observe animals for any sign of sickness or injury

5:30 P.M. Lock up enclosures before leaving

A special place to live

Each animal has its own special needs for shade, shelter, vegetation, water features, and landscaping. So zookeepers take care of all kinds of exhibits—aviaries, paddocks, aquariums, cages, and habitat boxes.

Keep your eyes on that eagle

We quickly discover that one of the kangaroos in the exhibit near the eagle exhibit somehow managed to make a hole in the mesh. This hole allowed the eagle to escape. Just like people, animals never cease to amaze!

I leave the hole open for now and leave out a pan of chicken and some fresh water. You never know—Ralph may just return to his exhibit by himself.

Meanwhile, the rescue team tries to follow Ralph, but it doesn't take long before they lose sight of him. They drive around, hoping to spot him, but see nothing. We alert local wildlife-rescue centers, residents, and businesses, in case someone spots him. All we can do now is wait.

How I Became a Zookeeper

Growing up, I always loved animals. My family had a dog, a cat, and a fish, but I was always collecting other animals and looking after them. Big or little, it didn't matter. I collected ants, bugs, butterflies, and lizards. I also had a rabbit, a parrot, and a duck. I was fascinated by each animal's behavior and finding out how best to take care of them.

Whenever school was out for vacation, my family would visit a park or zoo. We all had our favorite animals we wanted to see. My older brother liked the giraffes, while my little sister thought the pandas were cool. I loved seeing the chimpanzees.

When I was 18, I got a volunteer job at an animal shelter. That job was a good start, but I knew that I wanted to work with unusual animals when I got older. So I applied to be a volunteer at a local animal park.

I volunteered at the park for several years, and enrolled in an animal-management program in college. That was great, because I could put what I was learning in school to use. I was up for anything when I was volunteering. I wanted experience with all the animals.

When I finished my degree, I used my experience and qualifications to get a full-time job working at a zoo. Now it's my job to look after all sorts of exotic animals.

A zookeeper should ...

✓ enjoy working with animals

✓ be able to handle animals with confidence and patience

✓ make accurate observations about animal behavior and health

✓ have good communication skills

✓ be well-organized

✓ be able to work as part of a team

✓ have good problem-solving skills

Caring for animals is a great job because you never stop learning. When you become attached to the animals, it can be sad when they die. But the work can also be very exciting—like watching baby animals that were born at the zoo grow up and become adults.

The job has a lot of responsibility. The animals rely on you for food, shelter, and comfort. Their health and happiness are your priority, but it's a job that gives you a lot back—and you never know what's going to happen next!

It's a demanding job

Looking after animals means being physically active and on your feet. You will work outdoors in all kinds of weather and probably lift or carry heavy loads. Make sure you're up to it!

Remember, being a zookeeper isn't just about cuddling koalas. Animals also get sick and die, or they may bite you or otherwise hurt you. The work is often hard and dirty. You need to be realistic about what this job involves. Of course, that is all balanced out by the amazing rewards of the job. Pluses include animal births, watching out for the animals' well-being, and enjoying seeing them live happy, healthy lives.

Saving Wild Animals

I am also an assistant animal rehabilitator for the Society for the Prevention of Cruelty to Animals. The SPCA is run by volunteers who rescue sick, injured, or orphaned animals. These animals are either placed in foster homes (if they are domestic animals like dogs or cats) or rehabilitated and released back into their natural habitat (if they are wild animals).

To be an animal rehabilitator, volunteers usually need to work under a licensed rehabber for a certain amount of time, usually at least two years. Some states require that volunteers also pass a written exam to become licensed to care for wildlife. They also must be sponsored by an already licensed rehabber.

Volunteering is a great way to meet other animal lovers.

The rehab program teaches its volunteers about animal identification and rescue, handling, and release techniques. Animal rehabilitators also need to have a great deal of time available—caring for sick animals is a big commitment! Because I have a full-time job, I assist other volunteers with their rescues and don't rehabilitate any animals myself.

I'm careful not to become too attached to the animals I help look after. That way it is easier to release the animals when the time comes. It also lessens the chance of animals becoming humanized (too used to people), which makes it difficult for them to live independently in the wild.

Wildlife rescue

Most states have an organization that cares for wildlife. Anyone can rescue an animal, but in most states, you need to be over 18 years old and have a license to care for them. Call your local animal shelter, the state's department of natural resources, or SPCA to check the rules and regulations in your state.

The eagle is sighted!

Around lunchtime, a local resident calls to tell us that he has spotted an unusual-looking eagle in a tree near his house. Two keepers and I take nets, gloves, a transport box, and Ralph's favorite food (chicken) to entice him back to safety.

On first sighting, the feathers standing up on the back of his neck tell us that Ralph is scared and tired. Since he has never been out of the zoo before, Ralph doesn't know how to find water or food, so he is probably thirsty and hungry.

A keeper throws Ralph some chicken. He grabs it with his talons and flies off before we can catch him.

We follow in hot pursuit in the rescue car. Using binoculars, we watch to see where he lands. Calmly and quietly, we park the car and creep closer with the equipment and, most important, more chicken.

Ralph is a part of our zoo's Birds of Prey demonstration. During the show, he is always rewarded with chicken if he lands on his keeper's glove. One of the keepers decides to see whether this trick will work.

He puts on the glove to protect his hand and arm from the eagle's sharp talons, and holds out a piece of chicken. Suddenly there is a whoosh from the bushes and Ralph swoops down. In the split second he is on the glove, the other keeper captures him with the net—success! He is then put carefully into the transport box.

Back at the zoo, the exhibit is repaired while the vet checks Ralph for any injuries. After getting a clean bill of health, Ralph is returned to the safety of his exhibit.

PUN FUN   **Nature reserves are eagle opportunity employers.**

What the Zoos Do

Zoos educate people about animals and their natural environments. People see the animals up close—and can smell, hear, and sometimes even touch them.

Signs provide information about where each species comes from and how it lives. Teachers and guides give talks so people understand the animals better.

Zoos teach us how to take care of animals, both in the wild and in captivity. They help protect animals, too.

Many endangered species become part of breeding programs in zoos to save them from extinction. Animals like California condors, giant pandas, and lions have been bred in captivity and released into the wild.

Zoos also give the public an opportunity to be up close and personal with animals from all over the world, without trekking or traveling around the globe. In the United States alone, more than 100 million people visit zoos every year.

Globally, there are at least 5,000 endangered species, and at least one dies out every year. Some endangered species are:

- Black rhino
- Giant panda
- Snow leopard
- Beluga sturgeon
- Right whale
- Alligator snapping turtle
- Monarch butterfly
- American pika
- Gorilla
- Grey nurse shark

Who's Who at the Zoo?

Working in a zoo community
Lots of people work in zoos to make sure the animals are happy and healthy. They're also there to make sure that visitors have a good time. Here are some jobs in the zoo community.

Director/park manager

Every zoo has a director or park manager who is in charge. These people work with the government and the community to make plans for the zoo. They decide the types of animals that should be kept, and how many. They also oversee the running of the zoo itself, as well as the care of the animals.

Veterinarian

Vets check the animals regularly so they stay healthy. Zoo veterinarians are some of the most versatile of all vets. They have to be prepared for all kinds of problems and all kinds of animals—from an iguana with a sore eye to a hippo with a stomachache. There are strong networks of zoo vets and medical specialists who help each other when unique medical situations arise.

20

A veterinary technician assists the vet in the treatment and care of animals.

Education staff

Many big zoos have zoo teachers who work with students of all ages. They design programs for students to enjoy both at the zoo and back in the classroom.

Gardening staff

The gardening staff has the big job of keeping all the zoo plants healthy and attractive. Some exhibits take more work than others—the Congo Gorilla Forest at the Bronx Zoo has more than 400 plant species.

Maintenance

Some animals need artificial lights, heating, or air conditioning to stay alive. For example, lizards need to live in a hot, humid environment, while polar bears need a lower temperature and pools of water to swim in. So our carpenters, painters, electricians, and plumbers must keep everything in good working order.

21

A History of Zoos

1500 B.C.
Egypt's Queen Hatshepsut builds the first zoo. It includes African animals like lions, monkeys, and even a giraffe.

400 B.C.
Almost all Roman city-states have collections of animals. Scholars like Aristotle use the collections to study animal behavior. Other animals are used for Colosseum battles with gladiators.

300 B.C.
Ptolemy II of Egypt assembles an enormous menagerie of animals, including 2,000 golden-horned bulls, 23,200 horses, 24 lions, 16 cheetahs, and eight pairs of ostriches.

63 B.C.
Rome's Augustus Caesar maintains a menagerie of more than 3,500 animals, including more than 600 lions, tigers, and other large animals.

1500
Spaniard Hernán Cortés visits the zoo of Montezuma, the chief of the Aztecs. Montezuma's zoo employs between 300 and 600 zookeepers.

1752
Vienna's Schonbrunn Zoo is built for the Austrian emperor's wife. It opens to the public in 1765.

Queen Hatshepsut's collection of exotic animals was the first prototype for a zoo.

1794
The Menagerie du Jardin des Plantes in Paris is the first zoo founded for scientific and educational purposes.

1828
The Zoological Society of London founds a zoo in Regent's Park. By 1872, it has around 500 animals. Today the London Zoo is the largest zoo in Europe.

1859
The Philadelphia Zoo becomes the first established zoo in the United States. Admission is $0.25 for adults and $0.10 for children. A zoo laboratory opens in 1901, and a children's zoo in 1938, both firsts in the United States. In the 1930s, it becomes the first zoo to formulate special diets for its animals.

1861
P.T. Barnum displays the first captive whales, two Beluga whales, at his museum in New York.

1907
Carl Hagenbeck founds the Carl Hagenbeck Zoo in Hamburg, Germany. It is the first zoo to use moated, barless, open-air enclosures made to resemble natural habitats found in the wild.

1963
First baby panda bred in captivity is born at the Peking Zoo in China.

2006
Average zoo admission price in the United States is more than $10 for adults and $6 for children. The average visit lasts 3.5 hours.

PUN FUN

A kangaroo that can't jump is completely hopless.

Eat This!

One of my responsibilities is making sure each animal is fed a balanced diet. As much as possible, we feed the animals exactly what they would eat in the wild.

Zoos usually get their food from suppliers who specially package and prepare food for zoos. Food must be handled and prepared according to the U.S. Department of Agriculture's special standards and guidelines.

Zoos go through a lot of food—in one year, the Brookfield Zoo in Chicago feeds:

- 570,000 pounds of hay
- 100,000 insects
- 21,490 pounds of apples
- 12,000 earthworms
- 10,000 pounds of trout
- 7,200 goldfish
- 6,500 chicks

Where is it?

Keepers sometimes hide food from the animals and encourage them to look for it. This method, known as enrichment, stimulates the animals to behave as they would in the wild. An animal can spend up to half an hour working to find its food.

Vitamins and special pellets or cubes are sometimes added to an animal's meal. Making sure each animal gets the proper nutrition is important. Vitamins ensure that the animals are getting what they need to live, grow, and reproduce.

It doesn't take long for an animal to figure out whether food contains a vitamin or a medicine if it doesn't taste quite right. It's up to me to get creative in the kitchen and think of new ways to get the vitamins and medicine down.

Homemade meals

Zoos often breed their own food, such as grasshoppers, cockroaches, flies, mealworms, locusts, earthworms, rats, and mice.

Zoo Menu

Zoos develop their own food mixtures to match the tastes of their animals. Some animals' appetites also vary from season to season. Keepers know food must be interesting to the animals and given in the correct amounts, so they spend lots of time weighing, chopping, and preparing food.

Animal	Daily feedings (adult animals)
Birds of prey	
Condor	2 rats or 10 chicks
Wedge-tailed eagle	1 rat
Mammals	
Elephant	125 lbs. of hay
	10 lbs. mixed fruits and vegetables
	10 lbs. herbivore pellets
Giraffe	5 lbs. mixed fruits and vegetables
	50 lbs. herbivore feed
	hay
	dairy meal cubes
Kangaroo	kangaroo feed (protein supplement)
	alfalfa
	3-5 carrots
	browse (trees, grass, etc.)

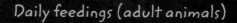

Daily feedings (adult animals)

7 ½ lbs. processed raw meat and
   6 cups dry kibble for males,
   3 lbs. processed raw meat and
   1 cup dry kibble for females
animal bones

mixed chopped fruit and vegetables
eggs
boiled chicken

2 teaspoons fly pupae
4 tablespoons mixed
   fruit and vegetables
dog kibble, crumbled
1 protein cube
native flowers
mealworms

diet varies according to size
   of snake

2 mice per week

7-8 rats per week plus 1 rabbit
   every 3-4 weeks

Food For Thought

Animals can develop health problems if given the wrong food. Tortoises' shells may become soft and flamingos can lose their color. Koalas will starve themselves to death if they are not fed the correct types of eucalyptus leaves. Penguins can get sick without enough salt in their diet.

When it comes to food, all animals fall into one of the following categories:

- carnivores: animals that eat only meat

- herbivores: animals that eat only plants

- omnivores: animals that eat both meat and plants

- insectivores: animals that eat only insects

There are also subcategories, including:

- piscivores: animals that eat fish

- frugivores: animals that eat fruit

- sanguinivores: animals that drink blood

- mycovore: animals that eat fungi

- mucivores: animals that feed on plant juices

The Frozen Zoo

San Diego's Center for Conservation and Research for Endangered Species has an incredible resource called the Frozen Zoo. Scientists collect cells from animals by taking a small notch of ear or skin during a routine vet visit. They then grow cell cultures of the animals' DNA in their laboratory and freeze them. In 2004, the Frozen Zoo had samples from more than 7,200 individuals in 675 species and subspecies.

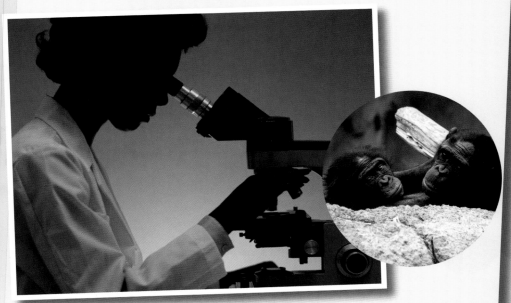

These samples are used to study genetic variation in populations of endangered animals, such as the gorilla and rhinoceros.

Scientists hope the frozen cells will help explain genetic problems. If an endangered animal's living cells are in the Frozen Zoo, they may be able to be used to prevent the extinction of the species.

Zoos Around The World

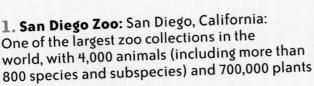

1. San Diego Zoo: San Diego, California: One of the largest zoo collections in the world, with 4,000 animals (including more than 800 species and subspecies) and 700,000 plants

2. Toronto Zoo: Scarborough, Ontario: Canada's premier zoo; one of the largest zoos in the world at 710 acres

3. Philadelphia Zoo: Philadelphia, Pennsylvania: Oldest zoo in the United States (1874)

4. Busch Gardens: Tampa Bay, Florida: Most visitors per year (4.5 million)

5. London Zoo: London, England: Oldest scientific zoo (1828)

6. Berlin Zoo: Berlin, Germany: Largest number of species in any zoo (1,500 species)

7. Vienna Zoo: Vienna, Austria: Oldest running zoo in the world (1752)

8. Tisch Family Biblical Zoological Gardens: Jerusalem, Israel: Emphasizes rare species native to Israel and animals from the Bible

9. Giza Zoo: Cairo, Egypt: Most densely inhabited by animals and plant species; features many African species

10. National Zoo: Pretoria, South Africa: Rated as one of the top zoos in the world

11. Beijing Zoo: Beijing, China: Features rare animal species from around the world

12. Australia Zoo: Beerwah, Australia: Run by the family of Steve Irwin, the "Crocodile Hunter"

13. Melbourne Zoo: Melbourne, Australia: Australia's oldest zoo (1862); modeled after the London Zoo

How Exciting!

The zoo is expanding its crocodile exhibit, and the zoo director has just told me that I will be on the study team. We will be going to northern Australia for two weeks to study crocodiles in their natural habitat.

I will also study other reptiles that we may bring back. Queensland alone has more than 400 native reptiles! Studying animals in their natural environment helps zoos better care for animals in captivity. It's also a very adventurous and exciting part of the job.

"Crikey!"

Known for his "Crikey" catchphrase, Steve Irwin, also known as "The Crocodile Hunter," was born in Australia in 1962. His parents, Bob and Lyn, were conservationists and shared their love for animals with their son. In 1970, the family opened the Queensland Reptile and Fauna Park. Irwin helped with the daily care, feeding, and maintenance of the animals.

In the 1980s, Irwin volunteered with a government crocodile relocation program, removing dangerous crocs from busy or residential areas. He performed his services for free; in exchange, he asked that the crocs be moved to the park. Eventually the park would house more than 100 crocs, all either caught personally in the wild by Irwin or his father or born and raised in the park.

In 1991, Irwin took over the animal park and renamed it the Australia Zoo. The zoo contains more than 1,000 animals and employs 550 staff members. Until recently, it was home to one of the oldest animals in the world, a 175-year-old Galapagos tortoise named Harriet. The tortoise died in 2006.

Also in 1991, Irwin married his wife, Terri. The first episode of the television show *The Crocodile Hunter* was filmed during the couple's crocodile-trapping honeymoon. The couple had two children—Bindi was born in 1998 and Robert in 2003.

In 2006, Irwin was killed while filming a documentary in Australia's Great Barrier Reef. More than 5,000 mourners attended the service at the Australia Zoo. Several memorial sites and wildlife funds have been set up in Irwin's honor.

Chimp Talk

Wild chimpanzees live in large communities of between 15 and 120 individuals. They communicate with one another through a complex and subtle system of vocalization, facial expressions, body postures, and gestures.

Read my face ... what am I thinking?

Speaking chimpanzee

Zookeepers who work closely with chimpanzees watch the chimps' facial expressions to figure out how the chimps are feeling.

Face 1

When chimps are angry, they open their mouths wide and show their teeth. They frown and their eyes get smaller just as ours do. They can also make their hair stand on end.

 angry

Face 2

When chimps are bored or tired, they do a great job of mimicking us!

 bored

Face 3

When chimps are surprised and interested, they open their eyes wide and drop their lower jaw, just as we do.

 surprised

Face 4

When chimps are happy and feeling playful, they make laughing noises. Their eyes get narrower and they show their bottom teeth. We grin in much the same way.

 happy

Group names

A group of meerkats is called a *mob* or a *gang*. Some other animal groups include:

- A *troop* of baboons
- A *leap* of leopards
- An *ambush* of tigers
- An *ugly* of walruses
- A *zeal* of zebras
- A *murder* of crows

Let's talk

Most zookeepers form a strong bond with their animals. The animals learn to trust and understand the routine of the zoo and their keepers. Although they never speak the same language, a zookeeper can often tell how an animal is feeling by:

- ✓ the way it walks
- ✓ the way it stands
- ✓ the look on its face
- ✓ the sounds it makes
- ✓ the condition of its fur or feathers

Behind The Scenes

Once I have delivered breakfast and cleaned all the enclosures, I take Kaya the koala to the weighing room and pull out her observation folder. I place Kaya in the weighing bucket. She has been going in it since she was a baby, so she doesn't find it strange.

She has lost another half pound. I bundle her up and grab her folder, which outlines her previous weigh-ins, what she is eating, and how she has been behaving. It's time to see the vet.

I call Eric, the zoo vet, who comes to visit Kaya. She clings to my shirt. I stroke her back and avoid any sudden movements, which would upset her more. I put her gently on the observation table as Eric gives her a once-over and goes through her chart.

Eric thinks that Kaya may have had a tick that caused her to lose her appetite. She has a lump behind her left ear where the tick might have been, but there is no sign of it now.

He looks in Kaya's ears and all over her body. There are no signs of scratches, bites, or other ticks. Eric takes a blood sample for testing. We decide that Kaya will stay in the zoo hospital until she starts improving and putting weight back on.

PUN FUN

Two silkworms had a race. They ended up in a tie.

Kaya's Progress

The vet gives Kaya various gum leaves to try. Koalas are picky eaters, and out of the 500 species of eucalyptus native to Australia, they may only like the taste of 20. Kaya begins to munch on some blue gum leaves, but stops after a few bites.

✓ The next day

Kaya's blood sample comes back normal, so there's no answer there as to why she is losing weight. The mystery remains. The vet decides to feed her a batch of high-quality peppermint gum leaves, a variety she has never tasted before, and guess what—she eats it!

✓ Next few days

Great news! Kaya's appetite is returning to normal and she's slowly gaining weight. She is chomping down peppermint and red gum leaves, and is definitely on the road to recovery. It might have been a tick bite that put her off her food, although the vet thinks Kaya might also have a case of the fussy eaters.

Just like people, koalas can get sick of eating the same thing all the time. Now that Kaya loves peppermint gum leaves, she'll be back with the other koalas by the end of the week.

What a relief. Her current love of peppermint and red gum leaves is noted in her folder. Being a zookeeper is constantly surprising.
I wonder what her next favorite gum leaf will be.

The Tour

Leading tours and talking to visitors is a part of the job that I had to get used to. I am much better with animals than with people! Even so, it is very rewarding. My groups get to find out how amazing animals really are.

Teaching is part of the fun.

We walk past the hippos and stop to admire our new arrival—Lizzie, the baby hippopotamus. I explain that hippos ooze pink goo to keep their skin from drying out when they leave the water. So Lizzie's gooey skin is the sign of a happy, healthy, hippo baby.

We watch as Lizzie takes a drink from her mother. Baby hippos, called calves, are fed by their mothers until they are about 8 months old. They stay close to their mothers until they are about 2 or 3 years old.

Then we go into the zoo's Wild Animal Care Center and watch as a keeper feeds a baby raccoon.

This baby, Rocky, is being raised by a keeper because his mother stopped paying attention to him when he became sick. When Rocky gets bigger and stronger, he will be reintroduced to his raccoon family again.

We pass the wedge-tailed eagle exhibit, and I point out Ralph to the group. Then it's time to hand them over to the next keeper.

With my part of the tour done, I begin to think about Kaya again. I'll pay her a visit after I finish my daily animal reports.

Practice Being an Animal Keeper Now

Smell

Listen

Look

Record keeping is something keepers do every day. In a notebook, make daily notes about anything you think is important about your pet. Write down what you see, hear, and smell. Your notes will help you if your pet gets sick.

Look at things like:

- Health
- Weight
- Behavior
- Diet
- Training

You can start developing important animal-keeper skills right now.

Notes go in here.

Make notes about:

✓ how your pets move—energetic? stiff? limping?

✓ how well they eat—quickly? carefully? favorite foods?

✓ how their fur, feathers, skin or scales look—dull? dirty? clean? shiny or smooth?

Know what they need

Keepers need to create a comfortable, relaxing, yet interesting environment, where an animal will behave naturally.

Look for things they like to eat and have in their environment. Do research to find out how the animal lives in the wild and what conditions best suit it.

Watch their diet

Animals need fresh water and healthful food, and you must know what can make them sick.

Always keep food and water clean, and save treats for special occasions. Watch how much your animals eat— you don't want them getting too fat or too skinny.

Clean up!

It is a keeper's job to keep the animals' areas looking neat. Get a nose that can handle cleaning up animal waste.

The yucky stuff

Keep an eye on the animal, and notice how often it relieves itself. You can tell a lot about an animal by its droppings, or feces, and urine.

Follow These Steps To Become a Zookeeper

Step 1

Science (especially biology) and math are important subjects in school. Good grades will help you to further your studies later on.

Step 2

In college, choose animal-related fields such as biology, zoology, botany, ecology, and conservation. Take as many of these classes as you can. Graduating with a degree in a science-related field is a big plus in competing for jobs.

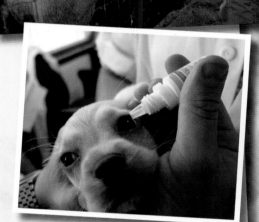

Step 3

Find opportunities to work with animals. Volunteer or get part-time work at pet shops, vet offices, a humane society, animal shelters, or farms or stables, or work for animal breeders.

Getting hands-on experience is an important step to becoming a zookeeper. Volunteer jobs or internships will give you a chance to handle and care for animals. Other jobs you might like include:

- Veterinarian
- Field researcher
- National park ranger
- Laboratory or animal health technician
- Animal trainer
- Zoo educator
- Wildlife officer
- Animal behaviorist

PUN FUN

Are evil wildebeests bad gnus?

Find Out More

- Jobs for animal caretakers are expected to grow faster than average. Pet owners are more interested in new services for their pets. But zookeeping jobs are expected to grow more slowly than other animal-care jobs, and are harder to find.

- Most zookeeper jobs require a bachelor's degree, and sometimes even a graduate degree, in biology.

- The U.S. Bureau of Labor Statistics estimates that there are more than 170,000 animal-care and service workers in the United States. However, fewer than 5,000 of these work in zoos.

- The U.S. Department of Labor estimates that average hourly pay for nonfarm animal caretakers, including zookeepers, is almost $10, or about $20,000 a year. The lowest 10 percent earn about $7 an hour, or about $14,000 a year. The highest 10 percent earn about $15 an hour, or about

Further Reading

Kehret, Peg. *Terror at the Zoo.* New York: Pocket Books, 1993.

Patterson, Caroline. *Who Pooped in the Zoo? San Diego Zoo: Exploring the Weirdest, Wackiest, Grossest and Most Surprising Facts About Zoo Poo.* Helena, Mont.: Farcountry Press, 2007.

Shenk, Ellen. *Careers With Animals: Exploring Occupations Involving Dogs, Horses, Cats, Birds, Wildlife, and Exotics.* Mechanicsburg, Pa.: Stackpole Books, 2005.

Zoehfeld, Kathleen Weidner. *Wild Lives: 100 Years of People and Animals at the Bronx Zoo.* New York: Alfred A. Knopf, 2006.

On The Web

For more information on this topic, use FactHound.

1. Go to *www.facthound.com*
2. Type in this book ID: 0756536162
3. Click on the *Fetch It* button.

Glossary

aviary—enclosure for confining birds

browse—leaves, shoots, branches, and other vegetation

botany—scientific study of plant life

captivity—unnatural environment in which animals are kept

cell culture—cells from plants or animals grown in a laboratory under controlled conditions

DNA (deoxyribonucleic acid)—found in the cells of all living things; passes on characteristics from parents to children

enrichment—mentally stimulating an animal to behave as it would in the wild

exhibit—display area surrounded by a fence or wall

extinct—died out; absence of a species because of hunting, environmental changes, or natural causes

genetic variation—variation of physical characteristics within a group or species; natural differences between living things

habitat—where an animal lives

humanized—accustomed to humans and human contact

invertebrate—animal without a backbone (such as insects)

kibble—wheat or grain ground into small pieces; often used as dog food

menagerie—collection of animals for study or display

nutrition—the taking in and use of food and other nourishing material by the body

paddock—fenced area for keeping animals

pupa—insect at the stage of changing from baby (larva) to adult (like a caterpillar in its cocoon before it becomes a butterfly)

rehabilitate—to restore to a natural condition; make well or better again

talon—claw, specifically one from a bird of prey

vertebrate—animal with backbone

vocalization—sounds an animal makes to communicate

Index

Look For More Books in This Series: